DEEP THOUGHTS FROM A SHALLOW GRAVE

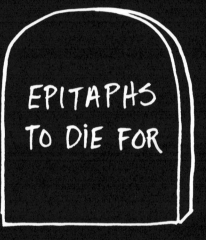

EPITAPHS
TO DIE FOR

ANTHONY MARTIGNETTI

RIZZOLI
UNIVERSE

IV

MY FINAL THOUGHTS ON LIFE
WILL HAVE TO BE INFERRED
THOUGH TO PASS THEM ON IN PERSON
WOULD BE VERY MUCH PREFERRED
ALAS THIS WILL NOT HAPPEN
SOMETHING GRAVE HAS THUS OCURRED
AND WITH ALL REMAINING THOUGHTS
I AM, FOR GOOD, BELOW INTERRED.

VI

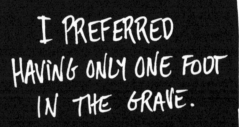

I PREFERRED
HAVING ONLY ONE FOOT
IN THE GRAVE.

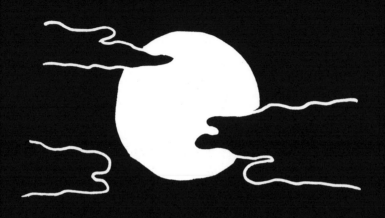

VIII

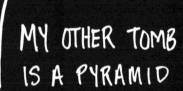

I WANTED A TOMB
WITH A VIEW

XIV

IF IT HADN'T KILLED ME
JUST IMAGINE HOW STRONG
IT WOULD HAVE MADE ME

CONTENTS NO LONGER
UNDER PRESSURE

WISH I WEREN'T
SO DOWN TO EARTH

XVIII

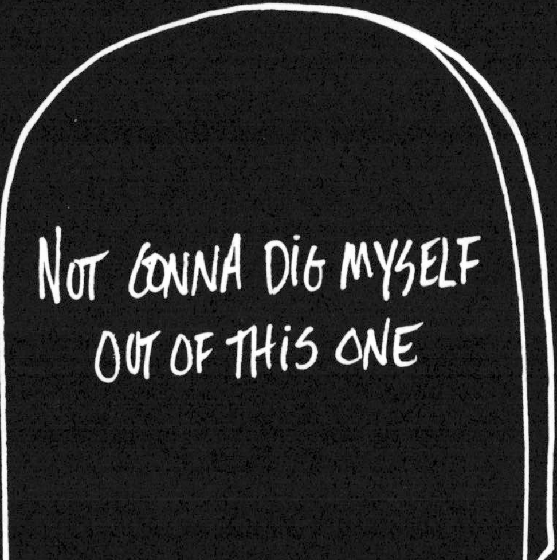
NOT GONNA DIG MYSELF
OUT OF THIS ONE

NOTHING IS CARVED
IN STONE

THINKING
INSIDE THE BOX

I TOLD YOU I WASN'T
FEELING VERY WELL

MY NEIGHBORS' KIDS
COME VISIT
EVERY WEEKEND

IT TURNS OUT
WHAT YOU DON'T KNOW
CAN HURT YOU

WAKE UP AND
SMELL THE COFFIN

READ THIS
AND WEEP

XXVI

OF THE MANY THINGS
I'D LIKE TO GET
OFF MY CHEST,
THIS PILE OF DIRT
IS THE MOST PRESSING

MY PLOT THICKENS

XXX

FINALLY -
NO ROOMMATES

I URNED THIS

XXXIV

THERE ARE FIFTY
BETTER WAYS
TO LEAVE YOUR LOVER

TALK ABOUT
A LIFE CHANGING
EXPERIENCE

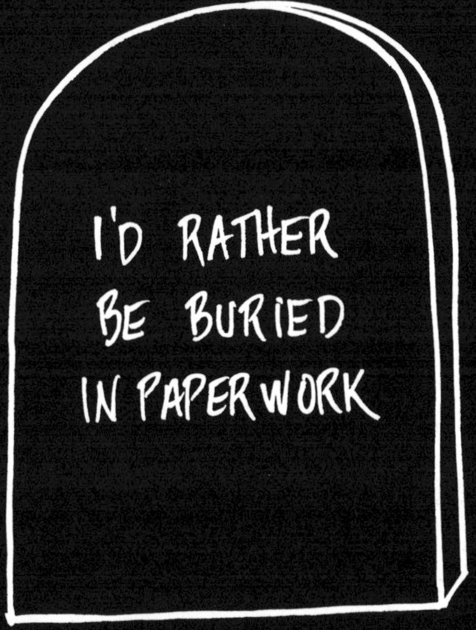
I'D RATHER
BE BURIED
IN PAPERWORK

I'M PRETTY MUCH DOWN FOR WHATEVER
I'M MORE OF A MOURNING PERSON
ALWAYS BEING THE LIFE OF THE PARTY WAS THE DEATH OF ME
PLEASE RESIST THE URGE TO DANCE ON MY GRAVE

THE DAY SEIZED ME

THE EARLY WORM GETS US ALL.

WAITING TO INHALE

I NEED A DEBOX.

XL

SEE YOU ON
THE OTHER SIDE.

NOT THIS
OTHER SIDE!
THE OTHER SIDE.

XLIV

· · ·

XLV

XLVI

THE SUSPENSE
FINALLY
KILLED ME

L

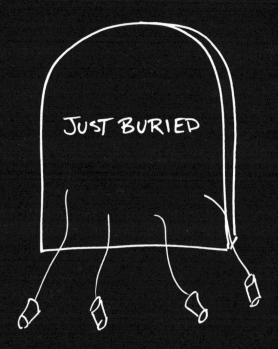

I COULDA BEEN
A COMMANDMENT

REFUSED AN OFFER
I SHOULDN'T HAVE

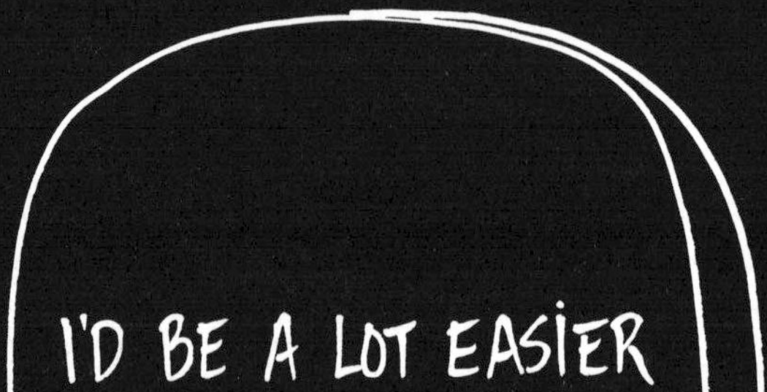
I'D BE A LOT EASIER
TO VISIT
IF YOU JUST KEPT ME
ON THE MANTLE

YOU CAN'T RISE
FROM THE ASHES
UNLESS
THEY CREMATE YOU

I SHOULD HAVE JOINED
THE RESISTANCE
INSTEAD OF
THE UNDERGROUND

I WENT BELOW
AND BEYOND.

PENCIL ME OUT

PER MY LAST EMAIL

YOU'RE JUST HERE
FOR THE
SCHADEN FREUDE

I'M DEAD TO YOU

UNDER & OUT

DON'T LET DEATH
GET IN THE WAY
OF A GOOD STORY

DEATH IS
A ONCE IN A
LIFETIME
OPPORTUNITY

BOUGHT THE DIP

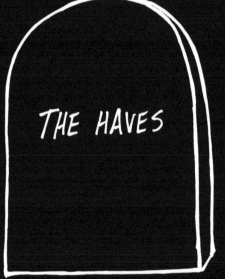

THE HAVES

THE HAVE NOTS

LXIV

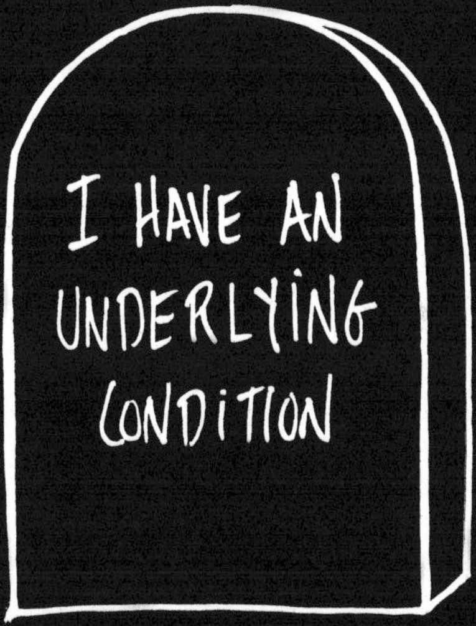
I HAVE AN
UNDERLYING
CONDITION

EVEN SCIENCE
REJECTED ME

DOES SOMETHING SMELL?
OR IS THAT JUST ME?

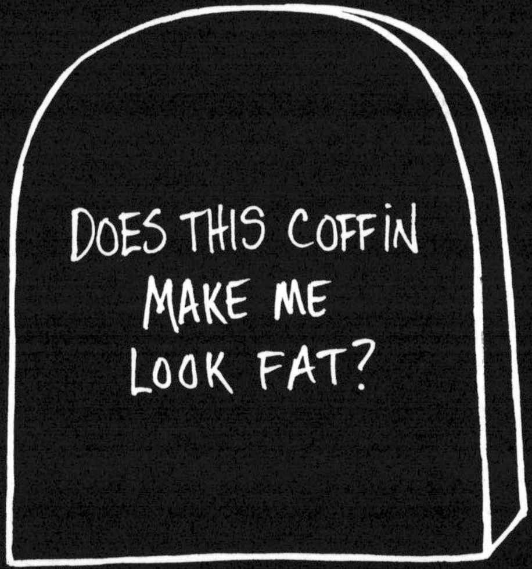
DOES THIS COFFIN
MAKE ME
LOOK FAT?

GRAVE NEW WORLD

LXXII

ACTUALLY
THINGS COULDN'T
HAVE BEEN WORSE

LXXIV

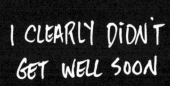

LXXVI

I HAVE NO PRETENSE
ABOUT BEING
PAST TENSE

YOU CAN KEEP
A GOOD MAN DOWN

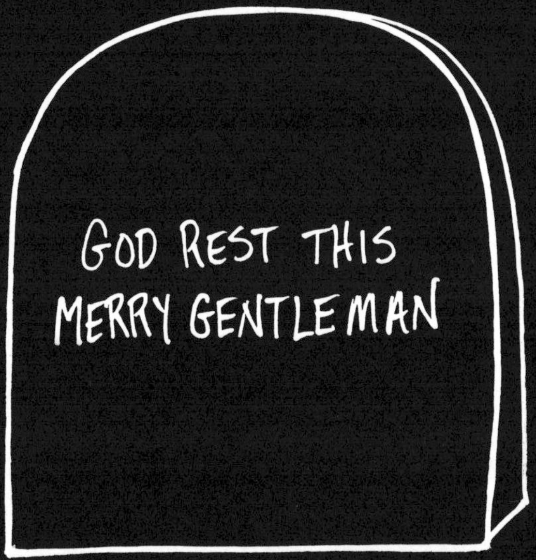
GOD REST THIS
MERRY GENTLEMAN

THE EARTH
SHALL INHERIT
THE MEEK

HELLO
MY NAME WAS

WHATEVER HAPPENED
TO FINALLY SLEEPING
WHEN YOU'RE DEAD?

PERMANENT
SAVASANA

I'M BETTER LATE
THAN EVER

FINALLY SOME LEGROOM

#METOMB

THERE'S PLENTY
OF DIRT
ON ALL OF US

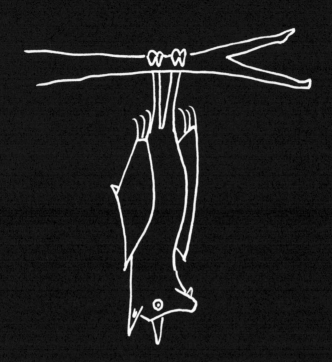

LXXXII

IF YOU'RE READING THIS
I'M PROBABLY DEAD

LXXXIV

I BLAME MY
PARENTS FOR THIS

I'M FEELING
A LITTLE BOXED IN

XC

AM I THERE YET ?

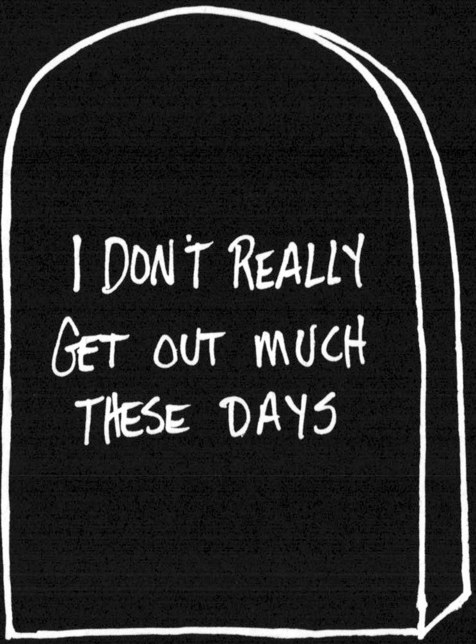
I DON'T REALLY
GET OUT MUCH
THESE DAYS

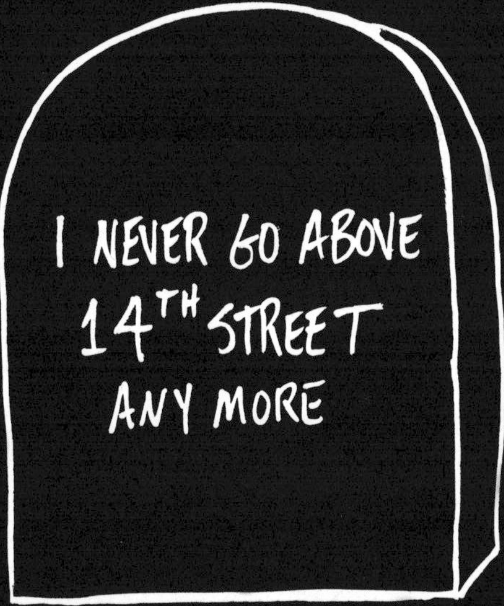
I NEVER GO ABOVE
14TH STREET
ANY MORE

XCIV

STARING OUT OF
THE ABYSS

MY SEDIMENTS
EXACTLY.

JUST SCRATCHING
THE SURFACE

FOUND MY
FOREVER HOME

INFERNALLY YOURS

CURRICULUM
MORTAE

MY END DID NOT JUSIFY MY MEANS
AN UNDERGROUND SENSATION!
NECROPHILIA JUST ISN'T AS FUN WHEN YOU'RE DEAD
THE ELEPHANT IN THE TOMB

C

C11

DEATH —
IT'S TOO TRUE
TO BE GOOD

CIV

ONCE THEY CLOSE
THE COFFIN
IT'S TOUGH TO SEE
THE SILVER LINING

CVI

GIVEN THE CHANCE
TO DO IT ALL AGAIN-
NEXT TIME
I WOULDN'T DIE

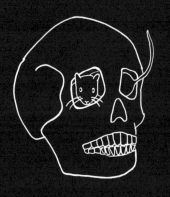

CIX

CX

I'LL BEGIN THE ACKNOWLEDGMENTS WITH ONE CENTRAL TO THIS BOOK... WE ARE ALL GOING TO DIE.
LET'S DO OUR BEST TO DIE LAUGHING.

NOW I WANT TO ACKNOWLEDGE SOME PEOPLE VERY DEAR TO ME. MOM, THANK YOU FOR YOUR (UN)CONDITIONAL LOVE AND FOR YOUR WONDERFULLY DARK SENSE OF HUMOR. AUNT MOLLY, YOU SHOWED ME THAT WITH A PIECE OF PAPER AND A SHARPIE, YOU CAN MAKE ANYONE LAUGH. ANITA, FOR ALWAYS LAUGHING AT MY JOKES – EVEN WHEN THEY AREN'T FUNNY. TOM, FOR NEVER LAUGHING AT MY JOKES – EVEN WHEN THEY ARE.

TO THOSE OF YOU WHO HELPED WITH THE TOMBSTONES DIRECTLY: THE BROTHERS SUGHRUE, ESPECIALLY JUSTIN, WHO HAD A HAND IN CARVING SOME OF THEM. CARL WEINBERG, BECAUSE EVERY DANTE NEEDS A VIRGIL. MY AGENT, MEG THOMPSON, WHO REFUSED TO CLOSE THE CASKET ON THIS BOOK. MY EDITOR, DANIEL MELAMUD, WHO GAVE IT A PROPER VIKING BURIAL. AND MOST OF ALL, ANGELA LEDGERWOOD, WHOSE BRIGHT SUNSHINE IS MY GUIDING LIGHT OUT OF THE UNDERWORLD IN WHICH I SO OFTEN FIND MYSELF.

TO THE NEW YORK NINES – MAY OUR CONVERSATIONS NEVER BE PUBLISHED...

TO THE REST OF MY DEAR FRIENDS, YOU KNOW WHO YOU ARE. THANK YOU FOR READING THIS FAR; I HOPE YOU ENJOYED IT. SEE YOU ALL ON _THE_ OTHER SIDE.

FIRST PUBLISHED IN THE UNITED STATES OF AMERICA IN 2024 BY
RIZZOLI UNIVERSE, A DIVISION OF
RIZZOLI INTERNATIONAL PUBLICATIONS, INC.
300 PARK AVENUE SOUTH
NEW YORK, NY 10010
WWW.RIZZOLIUSA.COM

EDITED AND DESIGNED BY DANIEL MELAMUD

PUBLISHER: CHARLES MIERS

PRODUCTION DIRECTOR: MARIA PIA GRAMAGLIA

PRODUCTION MANAGER: REBECCA AMBROSE

PRINTED IN CHINA ON FSC®-CERTIFIED PAPER
2024 2025 2026 2027 / 10 9 8 7 6 5 4 3 2 1
ISBN: 978-0-7893-4420-5
LIBRARY OF CONGRESS CONTROL NUMBER: 202 393 8876

VISIT US ONLINE:
FACEBOOK.COM/RIZZOLI NEW YORK
TWITTER @ RIZZOLI BOOKS
INSTAGRAM.COM/RIZZOLI BOOKS
PINTEREST.COM/RIZZOLI BOOKS
YOUTUBE.COM/USER/RIZZOLI NY
ISSUU.COM/RIZZOLI

FSC
www.fsc.org
MIX
Paper | Supporting
responsible forestry
FSC® C008047